Microsoft Word

The Microsoft 365 Companion Series

Dr. Patrick Jones

OLYMPUS ACADEMY
PRESS

TABLE OF CONTENTS

YOUR GATEWAY TO DOCUMENT CREATION

In a world where communication is often written before it is spoken, having a reliable tool for crafting your thoughts, ideas, and stories is indispensable. Enter Microsoft Word, the cornerstone of modern document creation. From crafting essays to drafting business proposals, Word has been the go-to platform for millions worldwide, revolutionizing how we write, edit, and share content.

But Microsoft Word is more than just a word processor. It's a versatile powerhouse capable of transforming a blank page into a polished, professional document. Whether you're a student formatting your first essay, a professional designing a complex report, or a creative writer weaving a compelling narrative, Word has the tools you need to bring your vision to life.

This book is your comprehensive guide to mastering Microsoft Word, from understanding its foundational features to exploring its advanced capabilities. More than that, it's a companion on your journey to becoming a confident and capable user of one of the most iconic tools in the Microsoft 365 suite.

You might be wondering, "Why should I dedicate time to mastering Word? Isn't it just a basic writing tool?" The truth is, Word is much more than meets the eye. Sure, it's where you write your letters and notes, but it's also where ideas take shape, stories come to life, and professional communication reaches new heights.

Consider this:

- **Professional Communication:** Word allows you to create documents that are not only clear and concise but also visually appealing and engaging.

- **Creativity Unleashed:** From resumes to newsletters, Word offers design features that let you showcase your personality and ideas.

- **Collaboration Made Easy:** With real-time editing and commenting features, Word makes teamwork seamless, even across time zones.

This book will show you why Word is more than just a tool—it's an essential skill in today's world.

In this journey, we'll explore Microsoft Word through a series of focused chapters, each designed to deepen your understanding and enhance your skills:

1. **What Is Microsoft Word?** Learn about Word's history, core features, and its role in the Microsoft 365 ecosystem.

2. **Why Use Microsoft Word?** Discover the unique advantages Word offers for personal, academic, and professional use.

3. **Getting Started with Word:** Step-by-step instructions to set up and customize Word for your needs.

4. **Best Practices for Using Word:** Tips for formatting, organizing, and optimizing your documents.

5. **Tips and Tricks:** Explore hidden gems, keyboard shortcuts, and advanced features to save time and add flair to your work.

6. **Copilot in Word:** See how AI-driven tools like Microsoft Copilot can revolutionize your document creation process.

7. **Common Pitfalls and How to Avoid Them:** Learn to sidestep common mistakes and keep your workflow efficient and frustration-free.

8. **Episode Example:** Follow a relatable story of how Sarah uses Word to tackle a challenging project, showcasing its features in action.

9. **Summary and Reflection:** Recap what you've learned and reflect on how Sarah's journey parallels your own transformation.

10. **Final Thoughts:** Tie it all together and look ahead to how Word integrates with the broader Microsoft 365 ecosystem.

Sarah, a marketing coordinator, didn't think much about Microsoft Word until her manager tasked her with creating an annual report for the company's stakeholders. At first, she felt overwhelmed by the sheer scope of the project. But as she explored Word's capabilities—templates, styles, and collaboration tools—she found herself not only completing the task but exceeding expectations.

Her experience wasn't just about learning features; it was about transforming how she approached her work. By mastering Word, Sarah gained confidence, saved time, and delivered a product she was proud of.

You, too, can experience this transformation. Whether you're a complete beginner or a seasoned user looking to refine your skills, this book will guide you step-by-step to unlock Word's potential.

Microsoft Word is more than just a tool—it's a skill that empowers you to communicate clearly, professionally, and creatively. It's a canvas for your ideas, a platform for your stories, and a bridge to your audience.

As you turn the pages of this book, you'll discover new ways to harness Word's features, streamline your workflow, and elevate your documents. But more than that, you'll discover the confidence that comes with mastering a tool that's central to modern communication.

WHAT IS MICROSOFT WORD?

Microsoft Word is one of the most iconic and widely used software applications in the world. For decades, it has been the cornerstone of document creation, editing, and formatting. But what exactly is Microsoft Word, and why has it remained a staple in homes, schools, and workplaces for so long?

At its core, Microsoft Word is a word processor—a program designed to create and manage text-based documents. Yet, to call it merely a word processor would be a disservice. Word has evolved into a sophisticated platform that combines powerful writing tools with advanced formatting, collaboration features, and integration with the broader Microsoft 365 ecosystem. Whether you're drafting a simple letter or designing a professional report, Word provides the tools to make your ideas shine.

Microsoft Word has undergone numerous iterations and improvements, adapting to the changing needs of users and the advancement of technology.

- **1980s:** Word debuted with features like WYSIWYG (What You See Is What You Get) formatting, setting it apart from other text editors of the time.

- **1990s:** Word became part of the Microsoft Office suite, gaining widespread adoption in both personal and professional settings.

- **2000s and Beyond:** With the rise of the internet and cloud computing, Word integrated collaboration features, allowing multiple users to work on documents in real-time.

Today, Microsoft Word is a central component of the Microsoft 365 suite, offering unparalleled functionality and versatility.

Microsoft Word is designed to cater to a wide range of needs, from basic writing tasks to complex document creation. Here's a closer look at some of its key features:

1. **Document Creation**
   - o Word offers a blank canvas for writing, but it's much more than that. With pre-designed templates for resumes, business letters, brochures, and more, you can create professional-looking documents without starting from scratch.

2. **Formatting Tools**
   - o From changing fonts and colors to adjusting margins and spacing, Word's formatting options allow you to customize your documents to look exactly how you want.
   - o **Styles and Themes:** Apply consistent formatting across your document with just a few clicks.

3. **Collaboration**
   - o Word's collaboration features, including real-time co-authoring and comments, make it easy to work with others, whether you're in the same office or halfway around the world.

4. **Reviewing and Editing**
   - o Built-in tools like Track Changes and Compare Documents simplify the editing process, making it easy to review revisions and ensure accuracy.

5. **Integrations**
   - o Word integrates seamlessly with other Microsoft 365 apps like Excel, PowerPoint, and OneDrive, allowing you to pull in data, share files, and work across platforms effortlessly.

One of Word's greatest strengths is its integration within Microsoft 365. This ecosystem connects Word with a suite of other tools designed to enhance productivity:

- **OneDrive:** Save and access your Word documents from anywhere, on any device.

- **Teams:** Share Word documents in Microsoft Teams and collaborate with your team in real-time.

- **Excel and PowerPoint:** Embed Excel charts or PowerPoint slides directly into your Word documents for seamless presentations and reporting.

This connectivity ensures that Word isn't just a standalone tool—it's a part of a broader system that makes your work more efficient and connected.

One of Word's most remarkable qualities is its versatility. It's used by people from all walks of life, including:

- **Students:** Writing essays, creating study guides, and formatting research papers.

- **Professionals:** Drafting contracts, preparing reports, and designing proposals.

- **Creative Writers:** Crafting stories, screenplays, or personal journals.

- **Educators:** Creating lesson plans, handouts, and syllabi.

No matter your profession or purpose, Word adapts to your needs.

Modern versions of Word have expanded far beyond simple text editing. Here are a few examples of its advanced capabilities:

- **Smart Features:** Tools like Editor provide grammar and style suggestions, helping you polish your writing.

- **Design and Layout:** Features like tables, charts, and SmartArt let you add visual elements to your documents.

- **Accessibility Tools:** Word includes features like immersive reader and voice dictation, ensuring it's usable by everyone.

- **Cloud Integration:** With Microsoft 365, your documents are saved automatically to the cloud, protecting your work and making it accessible from any device.

So, what makes Microsoft Word a tool that has stood the test of time? The answer lies in its combination of simplicity and power.

- **User-Friendly Interface:** Word is easy to use for beginners, yet packed with advanced features for experienced users.

- **Constant Innovation:** Microsoft continuously updates Word, adding new tools and improving existing ones to meet the demands of modern work.

- **Ubiquity:** Word's widespread adoption means it's compatible with most platforms and formats, making it a universal tool for communication.

Let's bring this to life with Sarah's story. Sarah had always used Word for basic tasks like writing letters and creating simple lists. But when she was tasked with preparing her company's annual report, she realized she had barely scratched the surface of what Word could do.

With some guidance, Sarah learned to use templates, styles, and collaboration tools. She even discovered how to embed Excel charts and design visually appealing layouts. By the time she finished the report, Sarah was not only impressed by Word's capabilities but also by her newfound confidence in using it.

Now that you know what Microsoft Word is and why it's such a powerful tool, the next step is to explore its benefits in greater detail.

WHY USE MICROSOFT WORD?

In a digital age dominated by communication and content creation, Microsoft Word stands as a trusted ally for crafting professional, polished, and purpose-driven documents. But why choose Word over the countless alternatives available today? The answer lies in its unparalleled versatility, user-friendly design, and seamless integration with the broader Microsoft 365 ecosystem.

This chapter explores the compelling reasons to make Microsoft Word your go-to tool, illustrating its transformative potential for personal, academic, and professional use. From simplifying your workflow to unleashing your creativity, Word empowers you to achieve more with less effort.

1. A Tool for Everyone, Everywhere

One of Word's greatest strengths is its accessibility and adaptability. Whether you're a student drafting a research paper, an entrepreneur preparing a business proposal, or a novelist penning your next masterpiece, Word has the tools you need to succeed.

- **For Students:** Word's citation tools, formatting options, and research integration make it indispensable for writing essays, theses, or study notes.

- **For Professionals:** From crafting reports and contracts to creating newsletters and presentations, Word ensures that your documents are both functional and visually impressive.

- **For Creatives:** Writers and designers can use Word's layout and design features to produce everything from manuscripts to marketing materials.

Example: Emily, a college student, used Word to write her senior thesis, leveraging its built-in referencing tools to save hours on formatting citations. Meanwhile, her dad, a small business owner, used Word to draft a contract for a new client.

2. Seamless Collaboration

In today's interconnected world, collaboration is key. Microsoft Word excels in enabling teamwork, even when contributors are spread across different locations or time zones.

- **Real-Time Co-Authoring:** Multiple users can edit the same document simultaneously, with changes visible in real time.

- **Commenting and Feedback:** Add comments and reply threads to facilitate discussion and review.

- **Track Changes:** Review edits made by others, accept or reject them, and maintain full control over the final document.

Example: A marketing team working on a campaign proposal can collaborate in Word, with the designer adding visuals, the writer refining text, and the manager providing feedback—all in one document.

3. Professional-Quality Results

First impressions matter, and Word equips you with the tools to create documents that stand out for their professionalism and polish.

- **Templates for Every Need:** Word offers a library of templates for resumes, letters, brochures, and more, saving you time and ensuring consistency.

- **Advanced Formatting:** Apply styles, adjust margins, and customize layouts to create documents that look as good as they read.

- **Design Features:** Add charts, tables, and SmartArt to make your content visually engaging and easier to understand.

Example: John, a job seeker, used Word's professional resume template to create a standout CV that landed him an interview. The recruiter even complimented the clean, well-organized design.

4. Time-Saving Tools

Efficiency is essential, and Word provides numerous features to help you work smarter, not harder.

- **AutoSave:** With cloud integration, your work is automatically saved as you type, reducing the risk of losing important edits.
- **Shortcuts:** Keyboard shortcuts for tasks like copying, pasting, and formatting save valuable time.
- **Quick Parts:** Reuse text or graphics by saving them as Quick Parts, eliminating repetitive tasks.

Example: A freelance writer used Quick Parts to insert her boilerplate email signature into proposals, cutting her prep time in half.

5. Integrated Research and Editing Tools

Microsoft Word isn't just about writing—it's about writing well. Its built-in tools help you research, refine, and perfect your content.

- **Researcher Tool:** Access sources and references without leaving Word.
- **Editor Feature:** Get grammar, spelling, and style suggestions to improve clarity and readability.
- **Translation and Accessibility:** Translate text into multiple languages or use accessibility tools like text-to-speech.

Example: Sarah, a non-native English speaker, used Word's Editor to refine her business presentation, ensuring it was clear and professional.

6. Connectivity Across Microsoft 365

Word's integration with the Microsoft 365 suite extends its functionality beyond document creation, making it a hub for productivity.

- **OneDrive Integration:** Access your documents from anywhere and share them with ease.

- **Excel and PowerPoint Compatibility:** Embed Excel charts or import slides from PowerPoint directly into your Word document.

- **Teams Collaboration:** Share and edit Word documents within Microsoft Teams for seamless teamwork.

Example: A project manager used Word to compile a project report, pulling data from Excel and formatting it into a polished document shared via Teams.

7. A Platform for Creativity

Word is more than a tool for professional communication—it's a canvas for creativity.

- **Layout and Design Options:** Customize your document's layout to reflect your unique vision.

- **Custom Fonts and Graphics:** Add personality with a wide range of fonts, graphics, and design elements.

- **Publishing Features:** Export your work as a PDF or print-ready document.

Example: A children's author used Word to draft her manuscript and design the layout for a self-published book, leveraging the platform's advanced formatting options.

8. Security and Privacy You Can Trust

In an age of cyber threats, Microsoft Word prioritizes the security and privacy of your documents.

- **Password Protection:** Secure sensitive documents with passwords.
- **Cloud Security:** Files stored in OneDrive are protected by Microsoft's robust security protocols.
- **Document Recovery:** Retrieve unsaved documents through Word's recovery feature.

Example: A lawyer drafting a confidential contract used Word's password protection to ensure the document remained secure until shared with the client.

9. A Tool That Grows with You

One of the most compelling reasons to use Word is its adaptability. Whether you're a beginner exploring its basic features or an advanced user leveraging macros and automation, Word evolves with your needs.

- **Beginner-Friendly:** Intuitive design and templates make it easy to get started.
- **Advanced Features:** Power users can explore macros, mail merges, and VBA scripting for even greater control.

Example: A student who started with Word for essays in high school later used it for project proposals in college and professional reports in their career.

In her journey with Word, Sarah discovered how this tool could simplify her workload and elevate the quality of her work. From drafting reports with advanced formatting to collaborating with her team in real time, Word became an indispensable part of her daily workflow.

Microsoft Word is more than just a word processor—it's a productivity powerhouse. Its flexibility, functionality, and integration with other tools make it a must-have for anyone looking to communicate effectively and work efficiently.

YOUR FIRST STEPS TO SUCCESS

Embarking on your journey with Microsoft Word doesn't have to be intimidating. While Word is packed with features, you don't need to master them all at once to start creating impressive documents. The key is to begin with the basics, explore at your own pace, and build your confidence as you go.

This chapter will guide you through the essentials of getting started with Microsoft Word, from setting up your workspace to creating your first document. Whether you're new to Word or refreshing your skills, this roadmap will help you hit the ground running.

1. Accessing Microsoft Word

The first step is ensuring you have access to Word. Since it's part of the Microsoft 365 suite, there are multiple ways to use it.

- **Desktop App:** The full-featured version of Word is available as a desktop application for Windows and macOS. Install it through your Microsoft 365 subscription or purchase it as a standalone product.

- **Web App:** Log in to Microsoft Word Online to use the browser-based version. While it offers fewer features than the desktop app, it's perfect for quick edits or working on shared documents.

- **Mobile App:** Download the Word app from your device's app store to create and edit documents on the go.

Pro Tip: For the most comprehensive experience, use the desktop app. Pair it with the web and mobile apps for flexibility and convenience.

2. Navigating the Word Interface

Once you open Word, you'll see its clean, user-friendly interface. Understanding its layout is the first step to working efficiently.

- **Ribbon:** This toolbar at the top of the window contains tabs like Home, Insert, and Design, each with groups of related tools.

- **Document Area:** The blank page in the center is where you type and edit your content.

- **Status Bar:** At the bottom, you'll find useful information like page count, word count, and zoom controls.

- **Quick Access Toolbar:** Located above the Ribbon, this customizable bar lets you add frequently used commands for easy access.

Pro Tip: Hover over any tool or icon to see a brief description of what it does.

3. Creating Your First Document

Let's start with the basics: creating a document.

- **Start a Blank Document:** When you open Word, you'll see the option to start a new blank document. Click it to begin with a fresh page.

- **Use a Template:** For pre-designed layouts, choose "New" from the File menu and browse Word's library of templates. Templates are great for resumes, reports, newsletters, and more.

- **Save Your Work:** Save your document early and often. Save to OneDrive for cloud access.

Pro Tip: Use descriptive filenames like "MarketingProposal_June2024" to keep your documents organized.

4. Customizing Your Workspace

Personalizing Word to fit your workflow can make a big difference in productivity.

- **Choose a Theme:** Go to File > Account to select a color theme for your Word interface.

- **Customize the Quick Access Toolbar:** Add commands you use often, like Print Preview or Save As.

- **Adjust Display Settings:** Use the View tab to switch between layouts like Print Layout, Web Layout, or Draft.

Pro Tip: Use Focus Mode under the View tab to hide distractions and concentrate on your writing.

5. Formatting Basics

Mastering basic formatting is essential for creating polished documents.

- **Text Formatting:** Use the Home tab to change fonts, font sizes, and text styles (bold, italic, underline).

- **Paragraph Formatting:** Adjust alignment, line spacing, and indents for clean, organized text.

- **Styles:** Apply pre-set styles to headings, subheadings, and body text for consistent formatting.

Example: If you're writing a report, use Heading 1 for section titles and Heading 2 for subsections. This also makes creating a Table of Contents easier.

6. Working with Files

Word provides flexible options for managing your documents.

- **Saving Options:** Save as a .docx file for full compatibility or export as a PDF for sharing.

- **Version History:** If you save your document to OneDrive, you can access previous versions.

- **Autosave:** Enable Autosave for documents stored in OneDrive, ensuring you never lose your work.

Pro Tip: Use the Save As function to create a duplicate of your file, leaving the original intact.

7. Adding Visual Elements

Make your documents visually appealing by adding images, charts, and other media.

- **Insert Images:** Use the Insert tab to add pictures from your computer or online.

- **Add Tables:** Create tables for structured data, like meeting agendas or budgets.

- **SmartArt and Charts:** Visualize complex ideas with graphics or charts linked from Excel.

Pro Tip: Use the Design tab to format your visuals, ensuring they align with your document's style.

8. Printing and Sharing

When your document is complete, Word makes it easy to share or print.

- **Print:** Click File > Print to preview and adjust print settings. Select options like paper size and orientation.

- **Share:** Use the Share button in the top-right corner to invite collaborators or send a link.

- **Export:** Save your document as a PDF for wider accessibility.

Pro Tip: Before sharing, use Word's Inspect Document feature (File > Info > Check for Issues) to remove sensitive metadata.

9. Exploring Templates for Efficiency

Templates are one of Word's most powerful time-saving features.

- **Find Templates:** Click "New" from the File menu to browse categories like resumes, calendars, or business plans.

- **Customize Templates:** Edit text, images, and styles to make the template your own.

Example: Sarah used a proposal template to create a client pitch, saving hours of formatting time and ensuring a professional appearance.

10. Experimenting with Word's Features

Getting started doesn't mean you have to stick to the basics. Word encourages exploration, so don't hesitate to try out new tools.

- Experiment with the Design tab to customize the look and feel of your document.

- Use the Review tab to explore tools like Track Changes and Compare Documents.

- Dive into the References tab to insert citations, footnotes, and bibliographies for academic writing.

Pro Tip: Start with one new feature at a time to avoid feeling overwhelmed.

Congratulations! You've taken your first steps into Microsoft Word and laid the foundation for effective document creation. Now that you've learned how to navigate Word, create documents, and customize your workspace, it's time to dive deeper into best practices for crafting professional, polished, and impactful content.

BEST PRACTICES FOR USING MICROSOFT WORD

Microsoft Word is more than just a word processor; it's a powerful tool capable of transforming your ideas into polished, professional documents. However, to truly unlock its potential, you need more than just an understanding of its features—you need a strategy. Adopting best practices ensures your documents are not only well-crafted but also efficient to create, easy to navigate, and visually appealing.

This chapter highlights tried-and-true methods to help you work smarter, save time, and produce exceptional results in Microsoft Word.

1. Plan Before You Type

The Best Practice: Before diving into writing, outline your document. Planning saves time and ensures a logical flow of information.

- **Example:** For a report, outline sections such as Introduction, Data Analysis, and Conclusion before starting.
- Use bullet points or headings in a rough draft to organize thoughts.
- If working with a team, finalize the outline collaboratively to align expectations.

Pro Tip: Use the Navigation Pane in Word to quickly move between sections once your outline is in place.

2. Use Styles for Consistent Formatting

The Best Practice: Styles are pre-designed text formats for headings, subheadings, and body text. They ensure consistency across your document and simplify changes.

- Apply Heading 1 for main sections, Heading 2 for subsections, and Normal for body text.

- Customize styles in the Design tab to match your document's theme.

Why It Matters: Using styles makes it easy to update formatting globally and creates a structure that's compatible with Word's Table of Contents feature.

Example: Sarah used styles in her annual report, enabling her to update all section titles' fonts with a single click.

3. Keep It Clean and Simple

The Best Practice: Resist the urge to overcomplicate your design. A clean, simple layout enhances readability and professionalism.

- Limit the number of fonts to two or three: one for headings and another for body text.

- Use whitespace strategically to avoid overcrowding the page.

- Align text consistently, and avoid unnecessary decorative elements.

Pro Tip: Use the Page Layout tab to adjust margins and spacing for a balanced appearance.

4. Use Templates for Repeated Work

The Best Practice: Templates save time and maintain consistency for recurring document types.

- Start with a Word-provided template or create your own for documents like invoices, letters, or project reports.

- Store frequently used templates in a shared folder for team access.

Example: A freelance writer created a custom invoice template, saving hours on formatting each month.

5. Leverage Document Sections

The Best Practice: Divide your document into sections for better control over formatting, especially in complex documents.

- Insert section breaks (Layout > Breaks > Section Break) to separate parts of your document.

- Apply unique headers, footers, or page orientations to specific sections.

Why It Matters: Sections allow you to include different layouts within the same document, such as landscape orientation for charts and portrait orientation for text.

Pro Tip: Use the Section Navigation in the footer to review and adjust settings quickly.

6. Master Collaboration Tools

The Best Practice: Word's collaboration features are essential for team projects.

- Use real-time co-authoring in documents stored on OneDrive or SharePoint.

- Track Changes to review edits, and use comments for feedback.

- Regularly resolve comments and accept or reject changes to maintain clarity.

Example: Sarah's marketing team used Word's collaboration tools to finalize a proposal, ensuring everyone's feedback was addressed before submission.

7. Optimize for Accessibility

The Best Practice: Make your documents accessible to all readers, including those with disabilities.

- Use Alt Text for images to describe their content.
- Choose high-contrast colors for text and background.
- Check accessibility using Word's built-in Accessibility Checker (File > Info > Check for Issues > Check Accessibility).

Pro Tip: Use headings and styles to structure your document, making it easier for screen readers to navigate.

8. Automate Repetitive Tasks

The Best Practice: Automation saves time and reduces errors in repetitive tasks.

- Create macros for tasks like formatting or inserting standard text blocks.
- Use Quick Parts to store frequently used phrases or graphics.
- Automate numbering for lists, headings, and captions to maintain consistency.

Example: A project manager used macros to standardize formatting for weekly reports, cutting preparation time in half.

9. Proofread Like a Pro

The Best Practice: Proofreading ensures your work is polished and free of errors.

- Use Word's Editor feature for grammar, spelling, and style suggestions.
- Read your document aloud or use Word's Read Aloud tool to catch overlooked errors.

- Print a copy for a final review, as mistakes are often easier to spot on paper.

Pro Tip: Customize Word's AutoCorrect options to automatically fix common typos as you type.

10. Prepare for Sharing

The Best Practice: Before sending or publishing, ensure your document is polished and secure.

- Use Word's Inspect Document feature (File > Info > Check for Issues) to remove hidden metadata or comments.
- Save as PDF for wider accessibility and to lock formatting.
- Use password protection for sensitive documents (File > Info > Protect Document).

Example: Sarah prepared her report for a client by converting it to a password-protected PDF, ensuring its content remained confidential.

11. Back Up and Version Control

The Best Practice: Avoid losing work by saving frequently and using version control.

- Save to OneDrive for automatic backups.
- Use Version History to restore earlier versions if needed.
- Name versions of your document clearly (e.g., "Proposal_v3_Final").

Pro Tip: Schedule regular backups of your files to an external drive or cloud service.

By adopting these best practices, you can take your Microsoft Word skills to the next level. These strategies will help you work more efficiently, create professional-quality documents, and collaborate seamlessly with others.

TIPS AND TRICKS FOR MASTERING MICROSOFT WORD

Microsoft Word is a powerful tool with countless features to explore, and even experienced users may not know all the ways it can save time and improve productivity. This chapter is packed with practical tips and tricks to help you get the most out of Word, from keyboard shortcuts to hidden features that can transform how you work. Whether you're looking to enhance your efficiency, polish your documents, or discover new capabilities, these insights will empower you to take your skills to the next level.

1. Customize Your Ribbon and Toolbar

Make Word work for you by customizing the Ribbon and Quick Access Toolbar with your most-used commands.

- **How to Customize the Ribbon:** Go to File > Options > Customize Ribbon. Add, remove, or rearrange commands to suit your workflow.

- **Quick Access Toolbar:** Add frequently used tools by clicking the drop-down arrow at the top-left corner of the window and selecting commands.

Example: Sarah added the "Track Changes" and "Insert Comment" options to her Quick Access Toolbar to streamline her editing workflow.

2. Leverage the Navigation Pane

For long documents, the Navigation Pane is invaluable for quickly moving between sections.

- **How to Open It:** Go to the View tab and check "Navigation Pane."

- **Features:** Use it to jump to headings, search for text, or reorganize content by dragging and dropping headings.

Pro Tip: Use styles (e.g., Heading 1, Heading 2) to populate the Navigation Pane automatically.

3. Automate with Quick Parts

Quick Parts allow you to save and reuse text or graphics, such as signatures, disclaimers, or logos.

- **How to Create a Quick Part:** Highlight the text or graphic, go to the Insert tab, click "Quick Parts," and select "Save Selection to Quick Part Gallery."
- **How to Use It:** Click "Quick Parts" and select your saved entry to insert it into your document.

Example: Sarah saved her email signature as a Quick Part to quickly add it to proposals and reports.

4. Use Word's Built-In Templates

Templates save time and ensure a professional look for documents like resumes, letters, and reports.

- **How to Find Templates:** Click "File," then "New," and browse Word's template gallery.
- **Customize Templates:** Modify fonts, colors, and layouts to make the template your own.

Pro Tip: Save customized templates for future use by selecting "Save As Template" under the File menu.

5. Protect Your Documents

Word offers several ways to safeguard your files, especially for sensitive or collaborative projects.

- **Restrict Editing:** Go to File > Info > Protect Document > Restrict Editing to limit changes others can make.

- **Password Protection:** Add a password to your document to control access (File > Info > Protect Document > Encrypt with Password).

- **Track Changes:** Use this feature for collaborative editing while maintaining control over final approvals.

Pro Tip: Use Word's Inspect Document tool (File > Info > Check for Issues) to remove metadata or hidden information before sharing.

6. Take Advantage of Research and Writing Tools

Word includes tools to enhance your writing and research processes.

- **Researcher:** Access credible sources directly within Word (References > Researcher).

- **Editor:** Use Word's Editor tool to catch spelling, grammar, and style issues.

- **Thesaurus:** Highlight a word and press Shift + F7 to find synonyms.

Pro Tip: Use Editor's settings to focus on specific improvements, like clarity, conciseness, or formality.

7. Explore Accessibility and Translation Features

Word's accessibility and translation tools make it easier to create inclusive documents for diverse audiences.

- **Accessibility Checker:** Review your document for potential barriers to accessibility (File > Info > Check for Issues > Check Accessibility).

- **Immersive Reader:** Enhance readability with tools like text spacing and line focus (View > Immersive Reader).

- **Translate:** Translate text into different languages directly in Word (Review > Translate).

Example: Sarah used the Accessibility Checker to ensure her client presentation was accessible to all attendees.

8. Make Use of Real-Time Collaboration

If your document is stored on OneDrive or SharePoint, Word allows real-time collaboration with others.

- **Share Your Document:** Click "Share" in the top-right corner to invite collaborators.

- **Use Comments and Suggestions:** Add comments to specific sections for team feedback.

Pro Tip: Use version history to revert to an earlier draft if needed.

9. Save Time with Smart Lookup

Need quick information or a definition? Use Word's Smart Lookup feature.

- **How to Use It:** Right-click on a word or phrase and select "Smart Lookup" to see definitions, web results, and related content.

Example: Sarah used Smart Lookup to confirm the spelling of a brand name while drafting a report.

These tips and tricks are just the beginning of what you can achieve with Microsoft Word. By exploring its hidden features and applying these techniques, you'll unlock new levels of productivity and creativity.

COPILOT IN MICROSOFT WORD

Imagine having a personal assistant embedded directly into your Microsoft Word workspace, ready to help you draft, edit, and refine your documents with ease. That's exactly what Microsoft Copilot brings to the table. By leveraging artificial intelligence (AI), Copilot transforms the way you interact with Word, automating repetitive tasks, improving the quality of your writing, and freeing you to focus on what matters most: your ideas.

This chapter explores how Copilot enhances the Word experience, walking you through its features, use cases, and tips for integrating it into your workflow. Whether you're a beginner or a seasoned user, Copilot can elevate your document creation process to new heights.

Microsoft Copilot is an AI-powered tool integrated into the Microsoft 365 suite. In Word, it acts as your writing assistant, offering capabilities that range from drafting and editing to summarizing and analyzing. Copilot uses natural language processing to understand your commands and provide intelligent suggestions, making it an intuitive and powerful ally for document creation.

Why It's Revolutionary:

- Automates mundane tasks like formatting and proofreading.

- Offers context-aware suggestions based on your document's content.

- Enhances productivity by reducing time spent on repetitive actions.

Think of Copilot as a collaborator—you guide it with clear prompts, and it helps shape your vision. To use Copilot in Word, you'll need an active Microsoft 365 subscription with Copilot enabled. Once available, Copilot appears as a sidebar within your Word interface, ready to assist whenever you need it.

Activating Copilot:

- Open Word and look for the Copilot icon in the toolbar.
- Click the icon to open the Copilot pane.
- Use the text box to input commands or ask questions.

Example Prompts:

- "Summarize this document in two paragraphs."
- "Draft a professional cover letter for a marketing role."
- "Format this section with headings and bullet points."

Pro Tip: Start with simple commands and experiment with different prompts to see how Copilot responds.

Key Features of Copilot in Word

1. **Drafting Content**
   Copilot can generate content based on your input, saving time and sparking creativity.

Example:

- o Prompt: "Write an introduction for a research paper on climate change."
- o Result: Copilot drafts a professional opening paragraph, which you can edit or refine.

Pro Tip: Use prompts that are specific and clear to get the best results.

2. **Editing and Proofreading**
   Copilot can review your text for grammar, spelling, and style, offering suggestions for improvement.

Example:

- o Prompt: "Improve the clarity and tone of this paragraph."
- o Result: Copilot rewrites the text, making it more concise and engaging.

Pro Tip: Pair Copilot with Word's Editor tool for comprehensive editing assistance.

3. **Summarizing Documents**
   Copilot excels at condensing lengthy documents into concise summaries.

Example:

- o Prompt: "Summarize this 10-page report into three key points."
- o Result: Copilot highlights the main ideas, saving you hours of manual review.

4. **Formatting Assistance**
   Copilot simplifies formatting, ensuring your document looks polished and professional.

Example:

- o Prompt: "Apply APA formatting to this document."
- o Result: Copilot adjusts margins, fonts, and citations according to APA guidelines.

5. **Inserting Visuals and Data**
   Copilot integrates seamlessly with other Microsoft tools, allowing you to embed charts, tables, or SmartArt.

Example:

- o Prompt: "Create a bar chart showing quarterly sales from this data."
- o Result: Copilot generates a chart and inserts it into your document.

Pro Tip: Combine Copilot with Excel for more advanced data visualization.

6. **Idea Generation**
   Stuck on how to start or structure your document? Copilot can offer suggestions and ideas.

Example:

- o Prompt: "Suggest three headlines for a newsletter about employee wellness."
- o Result: Copilot provides creative options to get you started.

Practical Use Cases for Copilot in Word

- **For Professionals:** Create polished reports, proposals, and presentations with minimal effort.
- **For Students:** Generate outlines, refine essays, and format citations with ease.
- **For Writers:** Brainstorm ideas, draft content, and edit manuscripts efficiently.

Example: Sarah, who was overwhelmed by the task of drafting her company's annual report, used Copilot to outline the structure, draft sections, and refine her writing. The result? A professional document completed in half the usual time.

Best Practices for Using Copilot

- **Be Specific:** The clearer your prompt, the better the output. Instead of "Write a paragraph," try "Write a paragraph about the benefits of renewable energy."

- **Review and Refine:** Copilot's suggestions are helpful starting points, but always review and tweak the output to suit your needs.

- **Combine with Other Features:** Use Copilot alongside Word's built-in tools like Styles, Editor, and SmartArt for maximum efficiency.

While Copilot is a powerful tool, it's important to recognize its limitations:

- **Context Dependency:** Copilot relies on the information provided. Ambiguous prompts may lead to less accurate results.

- **Human Oversight Required:** Always review Copilot's output for accuracy, tone, and relevance.

- **Complex Formatting Challenges:** While Copilot can assist with formatting, manual adjustments may still be needed for intricate designs.

Treat Copilot as a helper, not a replacement for your expertise and judgment. As Microsoft continues to enhance its AI capabilities, Copilot will only become more powerful and intuitive. Expect features like deeper integration with other Microsoft 365 tools, improved contextual understanding, and expanded language support.

Copilot represents the next generation of productivity, enabling users to achieve more in less time. By embracing this technology, you'll stay ahead of the curve and transform the way you work with Word.

Now that you've explored the capabilities of Copilot, it's time to put them into practice. Experiment with prompts, discover how Copilot can simplify your tasks, and see firsthand how AI can enhance your productivity.

COMMON PITFALLS AND HOW TO AVOID THEM

Microsoft Word is a powerful tool, but like any software, it's not immune to user errors and missteps. Even seasoned users can fall into habits or encounter challenges that hinder their efficiency and productivity. This chapter explores the most common pitfalls people face when using Word and provides actionable strategies to overcome them. By understanding these challenges, you can avoid frustration and make the most of what Word has to offer.

1. Overcomplicating Formatting

The Pitfall:
Applying too many fonts, colors, and styles can make a document look cluttered and unprofessional. Manually formatting each section without using styles can also lead to inconsistencies and wasted time.

How to Avoid It:

- Use Word's built-in Styles to maintain a consistent and polished appearance throughout your document.

- Stick to a simple font scheme—one for headings and another for body text.

- Leverage templates to start with a professional design that's already optimized for readability.

Example: Sarah's initial draft of her report had five different fonts and inconsistent line spacing. By applying Word's Heading styles and a cohesive theme, she streamlined the document's appearance in minutes.

2. Ignoring Document Organization

The Pitfall:
Writing without a clear structure can result in documents that are hard to navigate, especially if they're long or complex. Skipping the use of headings or relying solely on text blocks makes it difficult for readers to find key information.

How to Avoid It:

- Create an outline before you start writing, then use headings (Heading 1, Heading 2, etc.) to structure your document.
- Turn on the Navigation Pane (View > Navigation Pane) to organize and easily move between sections.

Pro Tip: Word can automatically generate a Table of Contents if you use headings, making navigation even easier for your readers.

3. Failing to Save Work Regularly

The Pitfall:
Not saving your work often—or saving it only on your local device—can lead to catastrophic data loss in the event of a crash, power outage, or accidental deletion.

How to Avoid It:

- Enable AutoSave if your document is stored in OneDrive or SharePoint.
- Save to the cloud for added security and access across devices.

Example: After her laptop crashed during a client presentation, Sarah was relieved to find her report intact on OneDrive thanks to AutoSave.

4. Overlooking Collaboration Features

The Pitfall:
Sending multiple email attachments or versions of a document for review can create confusion and duplicate work.

How to Avoid It:

- Use Word's Real-Time Collaboration to work with others on the same document simultaneously.

- Share a link to the document stored on OneDrive or SharePoint instead of emailing separate copies.

- Use Track Changes and Comments to provide and review feedback efficiently.

Pro Tip: Use version history to revert to earlier drafts if necessary.

5. Mismanaging File Sizes

The Pitfall:
Inserting high-resolution images, videos, or too many graphics can bloat your file size, making it harder to share or load.

How to Avoid It:

- Compress images before inserting them into your document (File > Info > Compress Pictures).

- Use links to online videos instead of embedding them directly.

- Delete unused objects or graphics from your document.

Example: Sarah reduced her marketing proposal file size by 70% by compressing images, allowing her to email it without issues.

6. Forgetting Accessibility Considerations

The Pitfall:
Failing to optimize documents for accessibility can exclude readers with disabilities and limit usability.

How to Avoid It:

- Use Word's Accessibility Checker (File > Info > Check for Issues > Check Accessibility) to identify and fix potential barriers.
- Add alt text to images and ensure headings are applied properly.
- Avoid using color alone to convey meaning; combine it with text or patterns.

Pro Tip: Use high-contrast color schemes and larger fonts for enhanced readability.

7. Relying Too Heavily on Manual Edits

The Pitfall:
Manually making repetitive edits, such as changing font sizes or applying bold text, is time-consuming and error-prone.

How to Avoid It:

- Use Find and Replace to quickly update text across the document.
- Set up Quick Parts for reusable text or graphics.
- Leverage Styles to apply consistent formatting across sections.

Example: Sarah used Find and Replace to update the name of a client in her 50-page document, saving hours of manual edits.

8. Overcomplicating References and Citations

The Pitfall:
Manually creating citations, footnotes, or bibliographies increases the risk of errors and inconsistencies.

How to Avoid It:

- Use Word's References tab to insert citations and manage bibliographies automatically.

- Choose the appropriate citation style (e.g., APA, MLA) from the dropdown menu.

Pro Tip: Pair Word with tools like EndNote or Zotero for advanced reference management.

9. Neglecting Security Features

The Pitfall:
Failing to secure sensitive documents can result in unauthorized access or data breaches.

How to Avoid It:

- Use Password Protection (File > Info > Protect Document > Encrypt with Password).

- Restrict editing permissions for shared documents (File > Info > Protect Document > Restrict Editing).

- Inspect your document for hidden metadata before sharing (File > Info > Check for Issues > Inspect Document).

Example: Before sending a confidential contract to a client, Sarah used Word's password protection to ensure only authorized users could open it.

10. Overlooking Version History

The Pitfall:
Accidentally overwriting or losing earlier versions of a document can lead to wasted effort and frustration.

How to Avoid It:

- Save your document to OneDrive or SharePoint to enable version history automatically.

- Access previous versions by clicking File > Info > Version History.

Pro Tip: Label important milestones (e.g., "Final Draft") in your version history to quickly identify them later.

By avoiding these common pitfalls, you can work more effectively and confidently in Microsoft Word. Small changes in your habits—like using styles, saving frequently, and leveraging collaboration tools—can lead to big improvements in your productivity and document quality.

SARAH'S MICROSOFT WORD MAKEOVER

Sarah sat at her desk, staring at her computer screen. Her task for the day was daunting: create a polished, professional annual report for her company's stakeholders. She had been handed a rough draft—a chaotic mix of text blocks, inconsistent fonts, and scattered data tables. As marketing coordinator, it was her job to turn this mess into a document that would impress her boss and the stakeholders.

Her first instinct was to feel overwhelmed. She had used Microsoft Word before, but only for basic tasks. Now, she needed to produce a masterpiece, and time was running out. Determined to rise to the challenge, Sarah decided to dive deeper into Word's capabilities.

Sarah opened the rough draft and immediately identified the issues. The document lacked structure, with random fonts and inconsistent spacing making it difficult to read. She also noticed that crucial data points were buried in dense paragraphs.

Her first step was to take a breath and plan. "I need to bring order to this chaos," she thought. She remembered the advice from her recent training session on Microsoft Word: start with an outline and use styles for consistency.

Sarah began by reviewing the content and outlining the key sections of the report: Introduction, Key Achievements, Financial Overview, and Future Goals. Using the Navigation Pane, she added headings to each section, applying Word's Heading 1 style for main sections and Heading 2 for subsections.

Instantly, the document started to feel more organized. The Navigation Pane allowed her to move easily between sections, making the editing process more manageable.

"I can do this," Sarah said to herself, feeling a spark of confidence.

Next, Sarah tackled the formatting. The random mix of fonts and colors was distracting, so she selected a professional theme from Word's Design tab. She chose a clean, modern style with a navy blue accent for headings.

Her boss walked by and glanced at her screen. "That's already looking much better," he said. Sarah smiled, motivated to keep going.

The report included raw data that needed to be presented in a more digestible format. Sarah turned to Word's Insert tab, where she added charts and tables to visualize key metrics like sales growth and customer engagement.

For the Financial Overview section, she imported an Excel chart directly into the document, ensuring the data stayed up-to-date with any changes made in Excel. She also used SmartArt to create a simple timeline highlighting the company's major achievements over the past year.

"This is so much easier to read," Sarah thought as she previewed the document.

With the structure and formatting in place, Sarah needed feedback from her team. She saved the document to OneDrive and shared it via Microsoft Teams, inviting her colleagues to review and comment.

Using Word's Track Changes feature, her team suggested edits and added comments. Sarah appreciated how easy it was to accept or reject changes, keeping the final version clean and professional.

Her teammate Lisa added a comment: "The Future Goals section could use more detail." Sarah responded within Word, asking for specific suggestions. The collaboration felt seamless, and the report was quickly improving.

As the deadline approached, Sarah decided to try Microsoft Copilot to refine the document further. She asked Copilot to summarize the Key Achievements section in two concise paragraphs. Within seconds, Copilot provided a clear, professional summary that Sarah only needed to tweak slightly.

For the Conclusion section, Sarah prompted Copilot: "Draft a closing statement emphasizing our growth and future potential." The result was impressive, capturing the tone she wanted while saving her valuable time.

With the content finalized, Sarah performed a final review. She used Word's Accessibility Checker to ensure the document was inclusive and readable for all stakeholders. She also ran the Spelling & Grammar check to catch any last-minute errors.

Finally, she exported the document as a PDF and added password protection to ensure it stayed confidential.

When the report was presented at the stakeholder meeting, it received glowing feedback. "This is the most professional report we've had in years," her boss said. Sarah felt a sense of pride, knowing she had transformed a chaotic draft into a polished document that represented the company's success.

Sarah's experience with Microsoft Word wasn't just about completing a project—it was about discovering the potential of a tool she had underestimated. By leveraging Word's features and adopting best practices, she saved time, reduced stress, and delivered a product she was proud of.

Her journey mirrors the one you're on as you learn to master Word. With the right strategies and a willingness to explore, you too can transform your work and achieve professional results.

SUMMARY AND REFLECTION: MASTERING MICROSOFT WORD

As we wrap up this journey through Microsoft Word, it's time to reflect on what we've learned and how it can transform the way you create, edit, and collaborate on documents. Microsoft Word isn't just a word processor; it's a tool that empowers you to communicate clearly, organize effectively, and present ideas professionally.

Let's summarize the key takeaways from this book and look back on Sarah's journey, which illustrates the practical application of these concepts. Her story mirrors the path you've taken in learning Word, providing a relatable and inspiring example of how to overcome challenges and achieve success.

This book has provided a comprehensive guide to Microsoft Word, broken into actionable, easy-to-follow chapters:

- **Introduction:** We set the stage by highlighting Word's importance in personal and professional communication and how it fits into the larger Microsoft 365 ecosystem.

- **What Is Microsoft Word?:** You explored Word's core features, its evolution over time, and its versatility as a tool for everyone— from students to professionals.

- **Why Use Microsoft Word?:** This chapter emphasized Word's unique strengths, such as collaboration tools, professional templates, and seamless integration with other Microsoft apps.

- **Getting Started with Word:** You learned how to navigate the interface, create documents, and customize your workspace to fit your needs.

- **Best Practices:** By adopting strategies like using styles, templates, and collaboration tools, you can streamline your workflow and produce polished documents.

- **Tips and Tricks:** This chapter unlocked hidden gems like Quick Parts and Smart Lookup to enhance productivity.

- **Copilot in Word:** We explored how AI-powered Copilot can automate tasks, improve writing, and provide intelligent suggestions, saving you time and effort.

- **Common Pitfalls:** Identifying and avoiding common mistakes ensured you could maintain an efficient, frustration-free workflow.

- **Episode:** Sarah's story brought these lessons to life, showing how Word's features can turn a daunting project into a triumph.

- **Final Thoughts:** We concluded by emphasizing Word's role as part of the Microsoft 365 ecosystem and encouraging continued learning and exploration.

Sarah's experience with Microsoft Word provides a relatable example of how to approach challenges and leverage tools to succeed. Her initial overwhelm with a chaotic report mirrors the uncertainty many users feel when first encountering Word's extensive features. But through persistence and exploration, Sarah transformed her task—and her confidence—by mastering the platform.

Let's revisit how her story aligns with the journey you've taken through this book:

1. **Starting with Hesitation:** Like Sarah, you might have approached Word with limited knowledge or hesitation. Her realization that planning and structure were essential reflects the importance of laying a strong foundation, as covered in the early chapters.

2. **Discovering Tools and Features:** Sarah's use of styles, templates, and the Navigation Pane illustrates how Word's features can simplify complex tasks. Similarly, this book guided you through these tools, showing how they can enhance your workflow.

3. **Collaborating and Refining:** Sarah's seamless use of Track Changes and real-time collaboration mirrors the focus on teamwork emphasized in the tips and best practices chapters. These tools allow for smooth communication and shared success.

4. **Embracing AI with Copilot:** When Sarah used Copilot to refine her content, she demonstrated how AI can save time and elevate quality. This mirrors the opportunities presented to you in the Copilot chapter, empowering you to use AI as a creative and practical partner.

5. **Delivering with Confidence:** Sarah's final report, polished and professional, represents the ultimate goal of mastering Word: delivering work that exceeds expectations. With the knowledge gained from this book, you're equipped to do the same.

Sarah's journey is a microcosm of your own path toward mastery. Both involve starting from a place of uncertainty, discovering tools and strategies, and ultimately achieving success through persistence and learning.

Like Sarah, you've explored the many facets of Word, from basic formatting to advanced collaboration and AI tools. Along the way, you've likely experienced moments of clarity, excitement, and empowerment as you unlocked new possibilities.

Ask Yourself:

- How has your understanding of Word evolved through this book?

- What features or strategies resonated with you most?

- How can you apply Sarah's approach to tackle your own challenges with Word?

While this book focused on Microsoft Word, it's only one piece of the larger Microsoft 365 ecosystem. The skills and strategies you've developed here can extend to other apps, enhancing your overall productivity and adaptability.

- Explore tools like SharePoint, OneDrive, and Teams to see how they integrate with Word.

- Continue experimenting with Word's features, especially those highlighted in the Tips and Tricks and Copilot chapters.

- Share what you've learned with colleagues or teammates to foster collaboration and knowledge-sharing.

Sarah's story is a reminder that learning is a journey, not a destination. By embracing challenges and seeking solutions, you can continue to grow and achieve your goals. Your willingness to explore Microsoft Word and apply its tools effectively is a testament to your dedication and adaptability.

The next time you face a daunting task, remember Sarah's transformation—and yours. With Word as your trusted ally, you have the skills and confidence to tackle any project and deliver results that stand out.

THE JOURNEY DOESN'T END HERE

As you reach the final chapter of this book, take a moment to reflect on how far you've come. Microsoft Word is no longer just a tool you use—it's now an extension of your creativity, organization, and professionalism. You've learned to harness its power to simplify complex tasks, collaborate effectively, and present your ideas with confidence.

But this journey is only the beginning. Word is just one part of the vast Microsoft 365 ecosystem, a suite of tools designed to work together to elevate your productivity and enhance your workflows. Each app offers unique features that complement Word, creating a cohesive environment where your skills and ideas can flourish.

Through this book, you've mastered the art of creating, formatting, and refining documents. You've discovered tools to collaborate seamlessly, explored the power of AI with Copilot, and learned how to avoid common pitfalls. These skills are not just about Word—they're about becoming a more efficient, effective, and confident communicator.

Word has provided you with a foundation, but growth happens when you apply what you've learned in new and unexpected ways. Use Word to:

- Draft compelling presentations that integrate with PowerPoint.
- Collaborate on detailed reports that pull data from Excel.
- Create structured documents that link to SharePoint for broader team visibility.

The more you explore, the more you'll see how Word interacts with the entire Microsoft 365 suite, empowering you to work smarter, not harder.

The Microsoft 365 ecosystem is vast, and each tool offers opportunities to expand your skills and productivity:

- **Explore SharePoint:** Learn how to organize and share information across teams, creating a central hub for collaboration.

- **Dive into Teams:** Discover how this communication platform integrates with Word to streamline teamwork and document sharing.

- **Master OneDrive:** Uncover ways to manage your files seamlessly, ensuring your Word documents are always accessible.

- **Embrace Copilot Across Apps:** See how AI transforms not just Word but also Excel, PowerPoint, and Teams with intelligent assistance.

Each of these tools is like a new chapter in your learning journey, offering ways to deepen your expertise and broaden your impact.

Technology evolves rapidly, and Microsoft Word is no exception. New features, updates, and integrations are introduced regularly, ensuring Word remains relevant in an ever-changing world. Staying curious and adaptable is key to maximizing its potential:

- **Keep Learning:** Follow blogs, tutorials, and forums to stay informed about new features.

- **Experiment:** Challenge yourself to use Word in different contexts, from creative writing to project management.

- **Teach Others:** Share your knowledge with colleagues or peers, fostering a culture of learning and collaboration.

Your journey with Word is part of a larger transformation. By mastering Word, you've not only improved your technical skills but also gained confidence in your ability to adapt, innovate, and excel. This transformation reflects a broader trend: the integration of technology into every aspect of work and life.

As tools like Word continue to evolve, you'll find yourself at the forefront of change, equipped with the knowledge and resilience to thrive in any environment.

This book is just one in the Microsoft 365 Companion Series, a collection designed to help you master each tool in the suite. If you enjoyed learning about Word, consider exploring the other books in the series:

- **Microsoft SharePoint:** Organize, collaborate, and share like never before.

- **Microsoft OneDrive:** Simplify your file management and storage.

- **Microsoft Teams:** Transform how you communicate and collaborate.

- **Microsoft Copilot:** Dive deeper into how AI enhances productivity across apps.

Each book offers a step-by-step guide to mastering another piece of the Microsoft 365 puzzle, empowering you to grow further in your digital journey.

Your decision to invest time and effort into mastering Microsoft Word speaks volumes about your commitment to personal and professional growth. The skills you've gained here are more than just practical—they're transformative. They position you as a leader, a communicator, and a creator in an increasingly digital world.

Remember, learning is a journey, not a destination. Each document you create, each feature you explore, and each new challenge you tackle is another step forward. So, take what you've learned, apply it boldly, and keep pushing the boundaries of what's possible.

Thank you for letting this book be a part of your journey. It has been a privilege to guide you through the world of Microsoft Word, and I hope it has equipped you with the tools and confidence to succeed.

The next chapter of your learning adventure is waiting—whether it's exploring other tools in Microsoft 365 or deepening your mastery of

Word itself. Whatever path you choose, know that you're capable of achieving great things.

Here's to your continued growth and success. The future is yours to write—so make it extraordinary!